Kindle Paperwhite User Manual: Guide to Enjoying Your E-reader! (Updated for 2013)

By Shelby Johnson

Disclaimer:

This eBook is an unofficial guide for the Kindle Paperwhite and is not meant to replace any official documentation that came with the device. The information in this guide is meant as recommendations and suggestions, but the author bears no responsibility for any issues arising from improper use of the tablet. The owner of the device is responsible for taking all necessary precautions and measures with the tablet.

Author Introduction

Hello, I'm bestselling Kindle eBook author, Shelby Johnson. Among the previous titles I've released are *Facebook for Beginners: Navigating the Social Network*, and *Kindle Fire HD User's Guide Book: Unleash the Power of Your Tablet!*.

I am a longtime technology enthusiast, and have also worked in the technology field. My previous work included helping seniors at a care center to learn to use the Internet and email basics. I've also worked as an IT project manager, helping to train employees on the use of various computer hardware and software. In case you're wondering, I also own a Kindle Fire HD and the new Paperwhite e-Reader (both 2012 and 2013 versions), and I love both devices for reading and other functions. I am not a salesperson or looking to give you a sales pitch for the item inside this eBook.

I have updated this manual to include all the new features of the Kindle Paperwhite Amazon released in October 2013. While many of the functions stayed the same, there are others that are brand new. This user's manual will work for both versions of the device.

In this new Paperwhite User Manual, it is my goal to help others to understand the basics of using their devices, as well as provide some other helpful tips and tricks. I have done my best to pack more into this book than you will see in the other Paperwhite guides on the market. Simply put, you're getting more than your money's worth with the comprehensive information provided in this guide! So let's get started on learning how to get the most out of the Kindle Paperwhite for reading and other functions.

Table of Contents

Kindle Paperwhite

Your Kindle Paperwhite will arrive from Amazon quickly. It comes in a nice, easy-to-open box. Simply grab the tab, and pull it open. Inside the box you will find the Kindle device, a white USB charging cable, and a little brochure called "getting to know your kindle."

Charging Your Kindle Paperwhite

Use the USB charging cable to connect your new device to a computer or other power source to charge your new e-Reader once you open it.

1. Plug the mini USB end into the Kindle Paperwhite
2. Plug the USB into a computer's USB port, or into a USB power plug.

Helpful Tip: *If, for some reason, you do not have access to a USB power supply or computer, you can use a micro USB charger from a cell phone or other mobile device to charge your Kindle Paperwhite.*

Note: *The Kindle Paperwhite will be fully charged in four hours when plugged into a computer with the USB charging cable. The battery will last up to eight weeks with 1.5 hours of reading each day, but battery life depends on daily reading time.*

Setting Up Your Kindle Paperwhite

Once your Kindle Paperwhite is connected to a power source, press the "power" button at the bottom of the device. When the screen comes on, gently tap the screen to get started.

NOTE: *To do this, simply tap the screen gently. A touch keyboard will appear on the screen. Use this keyboard to type. The screen is very responsive and needs just a gentle, but quick touch to navigate.*

Selecting Language

The first thing you will see on your Kindle Paperwhite is a screen that allows you to select your language.

1. Find your language on the list on the screen.
2. To select your language, gently tap your finger on your language.

Connecting to Wi-Fi

After selecting a language, your Kindle Paperwhite will prompt you to connect to Wi-Fi. Tap "yes" and the list of available Wi-Fi connections will pop up on the screen.

1. Tap to choose your connection.
2. If necessary, type in your Wi-Fi's username and password in the appropriate boxes.

Register Your Device with Amazon

If you bought your Kindle through your own account, it may arrive on your doorstep registered to your account. However, if it was given to you as a gift, you may have to deregister it from the gift giver's account and register it to your own Amazon account.

To Register

1. Tap "Register."
2. Enter your Amazon Account details if you have them.
3. If you do not have an Amazon account, you have the option to create one at this point.

NOTE: *You will need a payment source when creating a new Amazon account for any purchases you may make using your Kindle Paperwhite.*

To Deregister Kindle Paperwhite from Device

If your Kindle Paperwhite was a gift and comes registered to another person's Amazon account, you will have to deregister from their account, and register to your own.

1. Tap "Deregister."
2. Follow screen to register to your Amazon account or create a new Amazon account if you do not have one.

Note: *You can also change your registration on your Kindle Paperwhite at any time by tapping your options menu icon (three bars at top right of menu area), tapping on "Settings" and tapping on "Registration."*

To Deregister From Amazon Website

You may want to deregister your Kindle Paperwhite from a computer using your Amazon account.

1. Go to the "Your Account" drop down menu. (Where it says Hello and your name above).
2. Click on "Manage Your Kindle."
3. You will see a screen which lists your "Registered Kindles." The Paperwhite will be there along with the name of the Kindle which you can edit.
4. Go over to the "Actions" area and click on "Deregister." You will receive a pop-up to "Deregister this device."
5. Click on the "Deregister" button. After a few moments, the device will now be deregistered from that account.

Note: *In the "Manage Your Kindle" area on Amazon you can also choose to edit your Paperwhite's name (example: John's Paperwhite) or unsubscribe from special offers on your device.*

Setting up Social Networks

Keeping in touch with friends, family, coworkers, and long lost acquaintances has never been easier with the help of the Kindle Paperwhite. Whether Facebook, Twitter, or both sites suit your social networking fancy, each is easy to set up on your device. Although you are given the option to set up both initially, just after registering your device, you can defer the process until later. If you do wait until later, it is easy to return to the setup page to make it happen. Keep in mind, you must first have a Facebook or Twitter account before completing the following course of action.

Setting up Facebook and Twitter

1. From the Home page, select "Menu" and then "Settings."
2. Choose "Reading Options," followed by "Social Networks."
3. Tap the "Link Account" icon and follow the instructions for each category you are interested in linking to your Paperwhite.

Once you are connected, you simply tap on the social network's icon to interact in either forum. Now you can provide status updates and share information directly from your Kindle Paperwhite.

Getting to Know Your Kindle Paperwhite

Next, you will see a series of introductory screens that will explain some basic features of your new Kindle Paperwhite. The first screen shows you the difference between your "Cloud" and your "device." Amazon stores every single book you buy on your "Cloud," and you can also download books to your device using Wi-Fi or 3G (if you bought a Paperwhite with 3G), or you can download them using your computer, and the USB cord that came in the box.

Top Menu Bar

Once you have registered your Kindle Paperwhite, you will find yourself immersed in a number of opportunities that entertain, educate, inform, or that are just plain fun. No matter what you use your Kindle Paperwhite for, the one constant graphic you will see is the ever-present Top Menu Bar (pictured above). This Top Menu Guide is the key to navigating your new Kindle Paperwhite.

Home

Your Home screen will give you a snapshot of everything that exists on your Kindle, whether it is your library, social media connections, subscriptions to newspapers or magazines and blogs, or personal documents you have saved. No matter what it is, or where it came from, your Home screen will reflect its existence. To return to the Home screen at any time during the use of your device, simply tap the house-shaped icon, located at the very top left of the device, in the Top Menu Bar.

Back

The next icon on the menu bar is a backwards arrow or a "less than" sign – if you are mathematically inclined. This button will return you to the previous screen you were on at any time. This is perfectly handy for perusing the internet or book selections, because you can simply go backwards without initiating a completely new search.

Brightness Light bulb

There is an icon that looks exactly like a standard light bulb that allows you to adjust the brightness of the screen and its contents. This is great for users who enjoy their Paperwhite at the beach, in the evenings, or on the train, because it allows you to adjust the e-Reader's light source depending on the conditions you are in, so you never have to stop reading. In even better news, the brightness level you decide on does not dictate your battery life. Thanks to the special LED lighting composition of the Paperwhite, a bright light no longer means a drained battery!

Shopping Cart

Fourth in line of the Top Menu Bar is the unmistakable Shopping Cart icon. It is exactly what it looks like, and will take you to an endless source of material that is available for purchase on Amazon. Magazines, eBooks, and newspapers are just the start of your shopping cart excursion, so think big! This shopping cart will never get too full, so pile on the entertainment and information.

You checkout using your existing profile, and you have the option to use a credit card or PayPal option that can be saved to your device for later purchases.

Helpful Tip: *If you save your payment source, all you have to do is enter your password to approve future purchases, instead of entering all of your account information each time you want to buy something using your Kindle Paperwhite.*

Search

The next icon is the Search option, which is denoted by a magnifying glass on the Top Menu Bar. Once tapped, this feature allows you to look for available eBooks, periodicals, and other materials effortlessly. When searching is enabled, so is the keyboard. Simply enter a keyword, subject, title, author, or phrase that reflects the composition of your search, and the Paperwhite will display the matching results in seconds.

Helpful Tip: *If the choice you are looking for is not revealed immediately, try refining your search by using exact words or phrases to cut down on unrelated matches.*

Options List (three lines)

The Options List, or the three lines stacked atop one another at the end of the Top Menu Bar, represents your additional options, including settings, synchronizing capabilities, and parental passwords. Each of these categories has subcategories that allow you to manage your Kindle Paperwhite optimally. The options will change based upon which feature you're using on your Paperwhite (i.e. reading an eBook, using the web browser, etc).

Settings

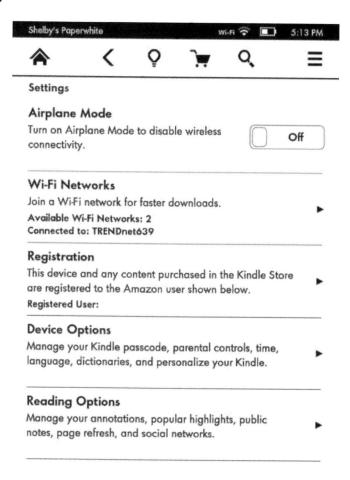

To review, modify, or revert to back to the original use of the Paperwhite, you will find just about everything you need under the Settings category, which can be found within the Options List (the three lines icon) in the Top Menu Bar. Once you are within the Settings, you can manipulate a number of options easily. Let's examine each of these options to see what they're used for.

Airplane Mode

While traveling, most airlines will ask that you use your electronic devices only during the approved windows of time (never while taking off, and never during landing) in Airplane Mode. This means that you can enjoy your device without interfering with the airplane's functionality, which is something that all travelers can appreciate. Simply change the setting to Airplane Mode during your travels, and slide it back to normal use once you are safely on the ground.

Wi-Fi Networks

When you are on the go, different Wi-Fi Networks will make themselves available for your use. With all of the hotspots available these days from your local coffee shop to friend's houses, simply tap the Wi-Fi list in Settings to display which ones are available to you at the time. The ones with a Lock icon next to them will require a password, which can be supplied from the source, meaning your neighborhood barista or your friend. Once you have returned home, you will need to display that functionality again to get back to your Wi-Fi network, and resume use of the device.

Registration

The Registration segment of the Settings simply allows you to see the Amazon account name that the device is registered under. You can also unregister your device in case of a transfer of ownership.

Device Options

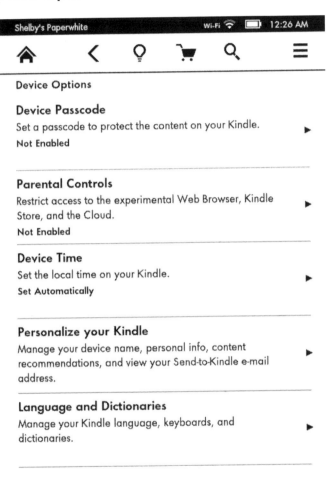

Device Options

Device Passcode

Set a passcode to protect the content on your Kindle. ▶

Not Enabled

Parental Controls

Restrict access to the experimental Web Browser, Kindle
Store, and the Cloud. ▶

Not Enabled

Device Time

Set the local time on your Kindle. ▶

Set Automatically

Personalize your Kindle

Manage your device name, personal info, content
recommendations, and view your Send-to-Kindle e-mail ▶
address.

Language and Dictionaries

Manage your Kindle language, keyboards, and ▶
dictionaries.

Device Options is a great way to keep your Kindle Paperwhite functioning optimally and specifically to your liking. It also allows you to ensure that others are not snooping around your contents, or making purchases on your behalf, without your knowledge. It also keeps the younger members of your household from viewing topics and information that are too mature their ages.

Device Passcode

Setting a device passcode is the perfect way to keep your Paperwhite to yourself. Once you set up a personal passcode, you will have to enter it to use the device, even when you wake it up from sleep mode.

Note: *Sleep mode is considered the time that the device goes dark during non-use, but is not turned off.*

It is incredibly important that you remember your passcode going forward, because this device does not offer an easy way to recover it. In fact, there is no recovery method. For most account passwords, you can request a change via email, or access a special link from the account. However, the Kindle Paperwhite requires a complete deactivation and reactivation of your account in order to provide you with a new password. This means that you will have to set up the device again, in its entirety, which will obviously be a pretty big hassle.

This is good to know for a number of reasons. First, it is important to back up all of your purchases, and downloads, so you can access them effortlessly in case of a passcode dilemma. Two, the Cloud should hold all of your contents, but you may want to search through it from time to time to familiarize yourself with its contents and filing procedures. This will help you re-download everything quickly and efficiently if you do have to deactivate and reactivate your account.

Be sure to take care of that password from the moment you choose it because it is not easy to get a new one if you forget it.

Parental Controls

If you have little ones, parental controls are a must. With the controls enabled, access to the Cloud is restricted along with access to the Experimental Browser and Kindle Store. That means no surprise downloads, and no awkward conversations resulting from questions about material little ones should have never seen to begin with. When children try and access the off limit areas otherwise, they will be prompted to enter a password to do so.

Helpful Tip: *Take care to choose a password that children will not figure out with a couple of different tries. Birthdays, anniversaries, and pets names are all too easy, and are not the most ideal way to go. Kids can be savvy, especially when it comes to electronics, and their ability to use them as they please.*

Device Time

This feature allows you to set the time on your Kindle Paperwhite, and is part of the registration process when you initiate the device. It also has the option to "Set Automatically," so it changes with your time zones when you travel, or after a jump in Daylight Savings Time.

Personalize Your Kindle

As you get acquainted with your device, you are going to want to make it your own, which is why the personalization option exists. You can name your device anything you would like, while entering your personal information including your name, address, or phone number, in case the device is ever misplaced or left behind at a café. Savvy technologists will know exactly where to look to find your information, and a Good Samaritan can return the device to you unharmed as a result.

The Paperwhite also has one of the best personalization features of any e-Reader called the "Send to Kindle" email address. This address allows you to input a specific address where documents and communications can be sent directly to your Kindle, and they are automatically formatted specifically for its use on the device. You will have to find another excuse besides, "I cannot open it!" when someone wants you to review a document when you are offsite.

Language and Dictionaries

This category is a fantastic addition, especially for any of the device's multi-lingual owners. Languages and Dictionaries allow you to choose which language your menus and instructions appear in, while providing access to a keyboard and dictionary of the same language. You can toggle between languages as you need to at any time. It is a perfect way to go from communicating in one language to another, without using two separate devices, keyboards, or software programs.

Reading Options

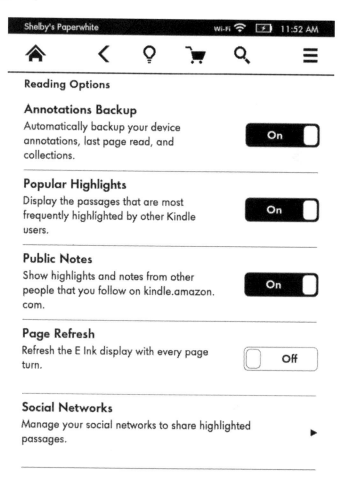

Now it is time to start reading and interacting with your Paperwhite! The reading options that are available on the device are unlike anything you would experience with a book's hard copy. Although at first glance there are features that are similar to jotting notes in the margins, you will immediately find that these options are so much more interactive, impressive, and helpful than anything you can do with a printed book.

Annotations Backup

Annotations are simply the comments, notes, or illustrative points that you make directly on the screen, within the material, as you read a book using your Kindle Paperwhite. The Annotations Backup allows you to turn the automatic backup of those notes, last page read, and collections within on and off to the Amazon Server. This feature allows you to make differing notes from the ones you have stored previously, in case this is your second time reading the book, or if you are simply referring to it for the tenth time.

Popular Highlights

This feature is a great tool for those who would like to see what others find worthy of being highlighted in the books across their library. You can turn this feature on and off, toggling between highlighted passages and not, to see what portions of the reading are most popular to others who have read it.

Public Notes

There is a Kindle Community where you can follow others who own the device, and they can follow you, if you are signed up for such interaction. It is a virtual, social network that is exclusive to Kindle owners. This community, in its entirety, can make notes and add highlights to the material they have read, and you can turn these notes on and off with this option.

The Public Notes option allows you to see what others are saying, and it provides you with insight that may not have existed before you read their comments. In addition, you can make your very own notes and accompanying highlights for others to explore your genius across a highly calculated group platform.

Page Refresh

This option allows you to reset the E Ink display each time you turn the page, so all of the interactive comments and highlights are available in real time. You certainly do not want to miss out on any comments or highlights that were made since you put a certain eBook down a week ago, do you?

Social Networks

If you have already set up your Facebook or Twitter (or both!) accounts, you can share passages, highlights, and insights from the material you are reading with your social networking community. So if you would like to drop one of your favorite passages from Romeo & Juliet into your Facebook status update, you can do so in a couple of quick taps of the fingers. The same goes for magazine articles, blog subscriptions, and newspaper columns.

How to Buy eBooks or Content on Your Paperwhite

You can buy content for your Paperwhite right from the device very easily. To do so, you'll need to be connected to a wireless network. Then, simply tap on the "Shopping Cart" icon on the Top Menu Bar. This will take you right to the Amazon.com Kindle store. From there, you can tap on various categories and options, or use the "Search box" at the top corner of the screen to find the particular eBook or content you want to buy.

When you tap on a particular book or other content, it will bring up the product page along with purchase options. You'll have the options to buy the book at its regular price, Borrow it for free (if you're an Amazon Prime member), Try a sample of the book, or Add it to your wish list.

How to Buy eBooks or Content at Amazon.com Site

If you prefer the traditional online shopping method of using your computer or laptop with an internet browser, you can still purchase content to add to your Paperwhite.

1. Go to the Amazon.com website and log-in with your account username and password.
2. On the left-hand side of your Amazon webpage is a vertical menu. Hover your mouse cursor over "Kindle" and then move it to the right to select the desired shopping location. This may include "Kindle Books," "Newsstand" and "Kindle Owners' Lending Library." You will be able to find, peruse and either purchase or borrow books within these categories. You must have a registered payment option in order to make purchases.
3. Once you have purchased an item on the Amazon website it will be stored in your free Amazon Cloud online. The online storage space allows you a certain amount of free space for every book, magazine, or other content you purchase. You can then access these items by tapping on the "Cloud" option on your Kindle.

For more information on finding books you've purchased, check out the "Where is the eBook I purchased?" **in the** Troubleshooting section.

Navigation of Books & Reading Options

While you're reading an eBook or other document on your Paperwhite, it's important to understand the various reading options you have at your fingertips. First, let's cover the basics of turning pages and accessing the menus or other information while reading a book on your device. Once an eBook or other document is open on your device:

1. To turn pages ahead, simply tap on the display screen towards the right side of the screen.
2. You can turn back a page by tapping towards the left side of the display screen.
3. To reveal the Top Menu of Reading Options (shown in the following image), while you are reading a book or document, simply tap quickly on the top of the Paperwhite screen.

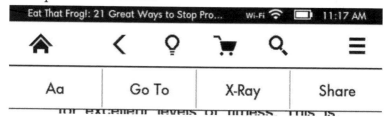

The Top Menu was covered earlier, but tapping on the three horizontal lines on this menu brings up a nice variety of reading options for your current eBook:

Shop Kindle Store – Tapping this option takes you right to Amazon's Kindle store so you can purchase new content for your device. You'll need to have a Wi-Fi connection enabled and a payment option stored with Amazon to do so.

Book Description – Tap on this choice to go to the Amazon book description page for the item you're currently reading. You'll need to be on a Wi-Fi connection for this option as well.

About the Author – On many titles tapping this option will pop up a nice little biography of the author(s) of your current eBook. It may also include additional Kindle eBooks that are available by the author(s), which you can tap on to view in the Kindle store.

Landscape Mode (or Portrait Mode) – Tapping on this option will allow you to change the orientation of your display. Landscape mode will present a longer side-to-side (left to right) display, whereas the Portrait mode is the typical book display with a longer top-to-bottom display.

Sync to Furthest Page Read – When you've purchased an eBook you may want to read it on several different devices such as your laptop, a work computer, online at Amazon's cloud reader, and on your Paperwhite device. Tapping on this option will synchronize your current eBook to the furthest page you've read. So if you've read ahead on a computer or wherever else you have your eBook, your Paperwhite will synchronize to that spot in the book, and you will never have to figure out where you were in a book.

Delete Bookmark – This option will simply delete any bookmark you may have made on the current page you are on.

View Notes & Marks – Tapping this option on many eBooks brings up some of the most popular highlighted portions of the eBook for you to view. These have been highlighted by other readers. Each highlight will include a snippet of the text, location and page numbers, and how many "highlighters" marked the passage.

Reading Progress – By tapping on this you'll bring up a pop-up menu with several progress display choices. You can choose which one you'd like displayed at the bottom of your eBook pages. They are:

- Location in book – this will now display the current location in the book you are on, at the bottom of your page display. Tap on the option to check it off if you'd like this as part of your page display.
- Time left in chapter – This will display approximately how much time it should take to finish reading the

particular chapter. Tap on this option to check it off, and the info will now display at the bottom of your eBook page. (Keep in mind this is not something that will cause the e-Reader to shut off if you don't finish in that time, it's just a suggested or approximate amount of time.)

- Time left in book – This will display how much time it should take to finish the eBook you are currently reading. The info will be shown at the bottom of your eBook's page now.

Settings

Other Reading Options Menu

Underneath that familiar Top Menu Bar that was covered earlier, there is another menu bar with four words or letters. This second menu holds some great features to help enhance your Paperwhite reading experience. Here are the details on how each of them helps to make your reading experience better. The following picture is what the menu looks like when you tap on the top of an eBook page, with descriptions of each option to follow.

Note: *To reveal this menu, all you'll need to do is tap the top of a page of an eBook or document you're currently reading.*

Aa	Go To	X-Ray	Share

Aa Fonts Feature

As mentioned before, by tapping on this particular option you can change the size of the font/text on your eBook or document to make it smaller or larger based on your preference. You also have at least six different fonts to choose from, and you are able to vary the document or eBook's line spacing and margins.

Go To Feature

The "Go To" menu option is helpful in terms of getting to a specific location in the book you're reading. By tapping on this, you'll open up a new menu that allows you to go to the Beginning of the book, a specific page or location, or one of the chapters inside the book. You may also be able to access the index and other sections, depending on what is included in that particular eBook.

X-Ray Feature

This feature is a nifty addition that you won't find in paperback books. By choosing X-ray from the Top Menu while you're on an eBook's page, you will be able to bring up all of the passages within that book mentioning a particular character, place, or topic of interest. As Amazon describes it, this feature lets you explore the "Bones of the Book." Keep in mind, not all books will have the X-Ray feature enabled, so don't become discouraged if this does not work for a particular eBook or document you are viewing.

Share Feature

The Share feature will allow you to type in a message regarding the eBook or document you're reading and then share it with either Twitter or Facebook. There will be a link to the book included when you share on Twitter or Facebook. Of course, you'll need to have one or both of these social networks connected to your Kindle Paperwhite in order to use this. Specifics on how to do connect social networks are outlined in earlier in the book.

Dictionary Feature (while reading)

after using **Reflexercise™**, some after only a few days. These folks experienced not only dramatic pain relief with their new exercise program, but also significantly reduced stress, anger, and

---

The New Oxford American Dictionary   ✕

sig·nif·i·cant adj. 1 sufficiently great or important to be worthy of attention; noteworthy: a significant increase in sales. 2 having a particular meaning; indicative of something: in times of stress her dreams seemed to her...

Show Full Definition

Highlight | **More**

While reading an eBook or document you can hold your finger down on a word to highlight the word and bring up the dictionary. A pop-up box will appear on your screen showing the word and its definition, with options for further analysis of that word in the dictionary. You can also choose to Show Full Definition, Highlight the word in your book, or tap on More options.

Note: *To highlight a word, you must hold your finger on the screen for longer than the tap you use to change the page or make selections. It may take some practice.*

By tapping on "More" you'll unlock further options including the option to share the word on Twitter or Facebook, the option to add a note with that word, the option to look the word up in the dictionary or Wikipedia, or the option to translate the word into another language. There is also the option to report a content error. This will help provide helpful feedback to Amazon and authors regarding typos, formatting or image issues, or other relevant problems.

Extra Reading Info (Bottom of Page)

tasks. High energy levels are		
1 min left in chapter		49 mins left in book
Loc 981 of 1647	Page 83 of 112	60%

When you're reading a page of an eBook or document and tap the top of your display, you'll also bring up some interesting information at the very bottom of your display, seen in the image above.

This other info is a statistical type view of your reading as well as other information including:

- How much time it should take to finish reading the particular chapter you are in.

- The location you are currently in for the eBook.
- The Page number you are on out of the total number of pages in the book.
- How much time it should take (approximately) to finish reading the book.
- Percentage of the book you have finished reading (or are at) so far.

Some individuals may find this information helpful for determining their progress with reading information quickly, or to find out a specific location they'll need to refer back to at a later time

Send to Kindle (for adding files to your e-Reader)

Send to Kindle is a very helpful way in which you can easily send content to your device, such as news articles, PDF documents, blog posts, or other documents you'd like to have on your device. For example, you may want to store e-mails, PDF's, recipes, directions, or instructions on your device for reference.

As of this guide book, you can send items to your Kindle Paperwhite from the Google Chrome or Mozilla Firefox web browsers, from e-mail, from a PC or Mac computer desktop, or from Android devices. When your Paperwhite is first registered, you will be provided with an e-mail address to use for sending documents to the device.

You can find that e-mail address by going to the Top Menu Bar on your Home screen, and tapping on the Options icon (three horizontal lines) at the far right of the menu. Tap on "Settings" and then tap on "Device Options." At the bottom of the screen you will see "Send-to-Kindle E-mail" info with the e-mail address to use to send documents to your device. It may be helpful to add this e-mail into your current e-mail contacts for future use.

You can find out more about this helpful feature at the link below:

Amazon send to Kindle
<http://www.amazon.com/gp/sendtokindle>

How to Transfer Content to your Kindle via USB (PC or Mac)

If you need to move documents from your Kindle device to your PC or Mac, you can do this rather easily by connecting your Paperwhite to the USB port on your computer with the included USB cable. Once it has been connected, you will see the Kindle as a drive option on your computer.

1. Plug the smaller end of the USB micro cable into your Kindle Paperwhite.
2. Plug the larger end of the USB micro cable into your MAC or PC.
3. Go to your computer's drives, files, and folders.

4. Double click on the "Kindle" to open the device and its folders on your MAC or PC.
5. Notice the "documents" folder that shows up in your Kindle. Simply drag and drop document files to that folder.
6. Unplug your Paperwhite from the PC or MAC (you may want to eject the device from the MAC before unplugging.)

Once your Kindle is unplugged from the computer, the document will appear on your device in the "Device" area.

Supported File Formats on the Paperwhite

The types of files you can store and access on your Paperwhite include the following file extensions:

.bmp
.doc
.epub
.gif
.html
.jpeg
.mobi
.pdf
.png
.txt

You will normally see these file extensions at the end of a file name on your computer. Several of the files mentioned above are image files (.png, .gif, .jpeg and .bmp). Keep in mind the Paperwhite displays in grayscale and some color images many not show up as well on the device. However, it is helpful to know that you can store text files (.txt), PDF's, HTML, .doc files from MS Word, and .epub or .mobi files in addition to the graphics files.

Create a New Collection

Collections allow you to sort the content on your Kindle as you see fit – without moving it from its original source. Since Collections are not files, you can put one article in two different places, or in five different places, if you would like. For instance, if gardening is a passion, you would create a Gardening Collection, and sort like material into it. You can create as many collections as you would like, The following steps explain how to create collections:

1. From the Home Screen, Tap "Menu."
2. Choose "Create New Collection."
3. Using the Keyboard, Type the Name of the Collection and Hit "OK."

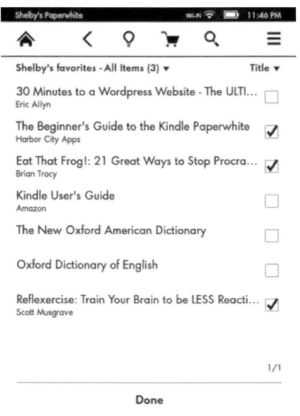

The device will generate a list of materials that can now be sorted into the collection (as seen in the image above). You should see checkboxes next to each of the listed eBook and document titles on your device which you can check off to add to the collection. Once you've checked of all the items you'd like in the collection, tap on "Done" at the bottom of the screen. The latest collection should now be showing on your display. You can tap on it to open and view all of the items inside.

It is important to note when creating a collection that blog subscriptions and periodicals are not applicable, and dictionaries – regardless of how many you download – will all be sorted under a dictionary collection automatically, and cannot be moved from that default collection.

Later on, if you would like to add and remove items, or to delete or change the name of any collection, at any time, simply apply your finger to the collection and hold it there until the Menu arrives, giving you all of the options you need to manage the collection accordingly.

Note: *If you delete a collection, the items stay on your Kindle Paperwhite, and are not deleted from your device.*

The Experimental Browser

The Kindle Paperwhite browser allows you to surf the web, and view most Amazon pages. However, it does not support media plug-ins (Adobe Flash), so videos, music, and other interactive stylings will not be available for your entertainment. A Wi-Fi connection is necessary to use this segment of the device.

Like other browsers you can bookmark sites, enlarge the page, and scroll up and down or side to side using your fingers directly on the screen. If you want to navigate the browser to a different site, tap on the navigation bar and the keyboard will appear. Enter the address you would like to view, and hit enter.

You can also search using keywords or phrases, if you do not know the address of a specific site. If you would like to enter information into a form, simply tap on the blank space on the actual web page, and the keyboard will appear to allow you to enter the information.

Going to a website

1. Tap the web address bar up at top of the screen.
2. Enter the desired site. Example: google.com
3. Tap the -> arrow to go to the site.

Note: *You may be prompted to connect to a Wi-Fi network, rather than using the 3G.*

Options

While you are inside the Experimental Browser, tap the Menu button to expose the following additional options to enhance your use of the device.

Article Mode

Article Mode is a no-nonsense application that allows a webpage article to be viewed in plain text columns, removing any images, credits, or ads from the article. This allows the content to be reviewed for exactly that: Content.

It is the perfect mode for research or information only articles, or if you generally want to speed up your viewing of an article or information on a particular webpage. Keep in mind it will work well on most webpages, but not perfectly on all.

Bookmarks

Bookmarks are saved online searches that allow you to keep a collection of web pages at your disposal, with the ability to access them with one tap. This function is ideal for websites you frequent, so you can simply select the bookmarks section, and tap the saved site all in a matter of seconds. Frequently bookmarked sites include Amazon.com, banks, news outlets, and blogs.

Bookmark this Page

The Bookmark this Page feature is helpful when you are using the Experimental Browser to view webpages on the Paperwhite. It will allow you to save a specific webpage to refer back to in the future. Here's how to do it:

1. Tap the Menu option (three horizontal lines icon) at top right corner of your screen.
2. From the dropdown menu, tap on "Bookmark This Page." The webpage you were viewing is now stored as a bookmark you can access in the future.

To Access Your Bookmarks

To access bookmarks when you use your Experimental Browser, complete the following steps:

1. Tap on the Menu option (three horizontal lines icon).
2. Tap "Bookmarks" from the list of options that show up.
3. Tap on any of the bookmarks you have stored on your Kindle. Once you tap on one, you will go to that webpage.

Edit or Remove Bookmarks

After step number two above, you can also edit your bookmarks. The following steps explain how to edit or remove your stored bookmarks.

1. Tap "Edit" to edit any of the stored bookmarks, or you can tap on "Remove" at the bottom of the screen and checkboxes will appear next to all of the bookmarks.
2. To delete bookmarks from your device, tap on the checkbox beside the bookmark you want to remove.

History

The History option will allow you to review each website you have previously visited. This is an easy way to refer back to something you found helpful before, without searching for the same link all over again. It is also a good way to see exactly what you or someone else has been looking up. So if you are planning a surprise party, those searches are going to appear in your History.

Helpful Tip: *As a good rule of thumb for all electronic device uses, assume everything you view online is listed in the browser's History.*

Browser Settings

Because the device does keep a running history of all of the sites you have visited, the Browser Settings menu allows you to delete the contents whenever you would like. In addition, the Experimental Browser runs a program called "Cookies" which saves and adds small bits of information to your device, based on the things you have researched, purchased, or perused. The "cookies" segment can also be deleted using the "Browser Settings." Lastly, the web segment of the device runs a source code called JavaScript, and an image provider. Both can be disabled, and by doing so the content on the webpages will inherently load faster.

Tap on the "Browser Settings" option to reveal the abilities to remove history, cookies and change your default settings for content downloaded. Some of these options, such as deleting cookies, will help as you've used the Web Browser over time and want to clean up excess files on your Paperwhite device, so that it performs faster.

Kindle Paperwhite

Troubleshooting

Let's face it: Technology giveth, and technology taketh away! Although the Kindle Paperwhite is easy to use, and makes a great gift for even the most novice electronics' user, there may be times when you need to troubleshoot an issue. In the case of this device, some are easy to detect and fix without any hassle or confusion.

Where is the eBook I just purchased?

If you've purchased an eBook and it was confirmed by the Amazon website, you will want to go to the Home screen of your Paperwhite device. Often times, books are stored in the Amazon cloud, which is your free online storage area. You will need to take some steps to find the book on the cloud, and download it onto the Paperwhite. Here's how:

1. From the Home screen on your device, tap on "Cloud" to see if the book is stored online with all of your other purchased content.

2. You can swipe your finger to the right side of the display to go to the next page full of content you've bought, or tap on "Recent" which will be part of the

menu near the upper right side of the display (it may say "Title" or "Author). "Recent" will display your most recent books purchased.

3. Tap on the particular book you want to add to your device. You may need to wait as it downloads the item, but it will now be found in the "Device" area of your Paperwhite.

4. If you are not seeing the eBook you just purchased in the Cloud, tap on the three horizontal lines icon in the top right of the display. On this menu tap on "Sync and Check for Items." The Paperwhite will now make sure all of your recently-purchased eBooks are updated in the Cloud.

   Note: *You will need a Wi-Fi connection in order to perform this operation.*

Device Frozen or Not Responding

Sometimes there is just too much going on with any device, and it finally just freezes as a result, for no rhyme or reason. If this happens to your Kindle Paperwhite, simply hold the power button for twenty whole seconds, and release. You will be presented with a reboot screen, and can get back to enjoying your device once it has cycled through the restart.

If that does not work, plug the device in so it is charged to at least forty percent battery capacity, and restart the device completely as listed above.

Device Not Charging

There could be a number of reasons why your device is not charging:

- The USB Cable is Not Fully Inserted (Check the Connection).
- The USB Cable is Bad (Use a New One).
- The USB Cable is Connected to an Older Source including an Antiquated Keyboard or Computer (Use an updated source).
- The USB Cable is Connected to a Non-functioning Port (Try another port).

Once you have ruled out any peripheral issues, try this:

- Ensure that the Device is Off & Not in Standby or Sleep Mode.
- Ensure that the Amber Light Indicator is Glowing (It will appear green, once fully charged).
- Disconnect the Source, and Restart the Device.

One of those items will get you back to charging in no time!

Device Not Recognized by Computer

If your computer does not recognize your device, try this:

From the device's home screen, select "Menu" and tap "Settings." Select "Menu" (yes, again) and tap the "Restart" button. Connect the device to your computer using the USB cord, and restart the computer.

If that does not work, try a different USB cord.

Device Not Opening Book

Sometimes items experience a troubled download, and unfortunately there is no way to know that until you are ready to enjoy them. If you device is not opening a book, try the following measures.

1. From your Home screen, select and hold the eBook that is not opening.
2. Select the "Remove from Device" option.
3. Locate and tap the Cloud tab.
4. Tap the eBook to download it again.
5. Restart the device once the eBook has completely downloaded.
6. Tap the eBook to open, and enjoy!

Can't Connect to Experimental Browser or Bookstore

If your Paperwhite is unable to connect to the Experimental Browser or the Amazon book store, your device may be offline. Use the following steps to resolve the issue:

1. Tap on the "Menu" icon at top right corner of your display (three horizontal lines).
2. Tap on "Settings" on the dropdown menu.
3. On the next screen, make sure "Airplane Mode" is set to "Off." Also, look at the "Wi-Fi Networks" option, which is the second option from the top. You will want to see if there are any available networks, and if you are currently connected.
4. If there are networks available, but your device isn't connected, tap on "Wi-Fi Networks."
5. On the pop-up box, you can tap on the available network, or tap on "Rescan" at the bottom to find any available networks to connect to.
6. Type in any necessary log-in information to connect with the Wi-Fi network and tap on "OK" to connect.

Keep in mind, if you are using your device somewhere that does not have an available Wi-Fi network, then you will be unable to connect to the Experimental Browser or Amazon bookstore. Those who have the 3G Paperwhite will be able to connect to the Amazon bookstore from anywhere they have a 3G signal.

Forgotten Password

If you forget your Kindle Paperwhite password, do not beat yourself up too badly. After all, you were warned that this would happen! After you forget it once, and go through the following steps, chances are you will never, ever forget it again. You live, you learn, and unfortunately this lesson comes with the necessity of a complete restoration of your device.

Once you have absolutely forgotten your password, you will need to restore your device to its original state, all the way back to the factory defaults. This will delete all of your content, and deregisters your device, so you will have to download everything again. Yes – this is the only way.

To do so, enter the numbers 111222777 where your password goes. The process will begin on its own, and you will need to retrieve everything that was on the device from the Cloud, and re-enter all of your personal information, purchasing profiles, and favorites all over again. Sorry.

Changing the Language Issue

At some point, your Kindle Paperwhite may inadvertently get set to a different language and you want to change it back to your preferred language. For example, someone may accidentally set your Paperwhite to Chinese rather than English. It will be incredibly difficult to fix because it is likely that you do not read Chinese. I have provide steps below that help by telling you what options you need to tap in each area until your Paperwhite is set back in English.

Here are the steps to fix that issue:

1. Tap the Menu icon at the top right corner of your display (the three horizontal lines).
2. On the drop-down menu, count down to the sixth option listed and tap on it (Settings).
3. On the next screen, count down the list to the fourth option listed and tap it (Device Options).
4. On the next screen, count down to the fifth option listed and tap on it (Language and Dictionaries).
5. On the next screen, tap on the first option listed (Languages).
6. You now will see a listing of all available languages. Tap on your preferred language so that the circle next to it is highlighted, then tap on "OK" at the bottom right of your display.

7. A box will pop up and will probably be in the other language, but tap on "OK" to restart your device in your new preferred language.
8. Allow several moments for your device to restart and it should now reflect the preferred language.

Opting out of Special Offers

When you first bought your Kindle Paperwhite you had the option to buy an ad-supported version for less money. If you have one of these devices and find the ads to become too obtrusive, you can choose to opt out of the ads, but it will cost you $15. You can learn the exact steps to unsubscribe from offers on your Kindle at the Amazon.com Unsubscribing from Offers page.
<http://www.amazon.com/gp/help/customer/display.html/ref=hp_special_unsubscribe?nodeId=200671290#unsubscribe>

Kindle Paperwhite Tips and Tricks

There are a number of tips and tricks to getting the most out of your Kindle Paperwhite. Although you will learn more as you go along and start using your device regularly, there are some that will help you right away.

Kindle Paperwhite Power Saving Tips

In an effort to save battery power on your device, place it in sleep mode when it is not in use. A fun fact about the Paperwhite is that sleep mode provides the same battery saving power as the off mode, so use it to your advantage. In addition, no matter which brightness selection you choose, the battery life will not be compromised, thanks to its efficient, low-power LED light source.

How to Touch Kindle Paperwhite Screen

Touch screens are very temperamental, and absolutely do not navigate more efficiently the harder you press, tap or bang on them! It takes a little getting used to, but when you are handling your device, do so softly and gently.

There are three basic touch zones on the Paperwhite, which are the right side of the page, the top one-inch section (Top Menu Bar) and the left side of the page. The types of touches the screen responds to are called a tap, a swipe, or a hold.

A tap is a single quick touch of the screen near the word or area you are trying to select. If you use a tap to the right while reading, you will page forward one page in a book, and if you tap to the left in an eBook, you will page back one page.

The icons and menus will all respond to a single tap, and screens can be navigated with the swipe of a finger from left to right, or up and down. The keyboard automatically reveals itself at any time there is a need to type, including searches, forms, and website addresses. The keys can be used just like a regular keyboard, and respond with a light tapping motion. To reveal numbers or symbols simply tap the "123" key.

As for a hold, you place your finger on the screen and leave it down longer than a tap. Typically this will highlight a word or phrase.

How to Backup Kindle Paperwhite to Amazon Cloud

You may have documents and other books on your Paperwhite that you did not buy from Amazon. If this is the case, they are not automatically stored to your free Amazon Cloud service. If you want to make sure a document is on your Cloud, you must send it to your Send to Kindle address or use Send to Kindle for PC, Mac or Web Browsers.

Instructions for Send to Kindle are available in an earlier section of this book.

Note: *The documents you send must be a Kindle Paperwhite supported file type if you want to be able to read them on your device.*

How to Backup Kindle Paperwhite to a Computer

Just in case the Amazon Cloud is not enough of a backup for your Kindle Paperwhite documents, another backup method could be your computer. This will help in the event that you forget your password and have to reset your device entirely. A simple way to backup your Kindle Paperwhite to your computer is similar to the reverse of How to Transfer Content to Your Kindle Via USB (PC or MAC).

1. Plug the smaller end of the USB micro cable into your Kindle Paperwhite.
2. Plug the larger end of the USB micro cable into your MAC or PC.
3. Go to your computer's drives, files, and folders.
4. Double click on the "Kindle" to open the device and its folders on your MAC or PC.
5. Notice the "documents" folder that shows up in your Kindle. Simply drag and drop the entire folder onto your computer.
   Helpful Tip: *If you would like, you could re-name this folder "Kindle Paperwhite" or whatever name you want once it is on your computer.*

This method will contain every document you have on your Kindle Paperwhite at the time you did the backup. If you purchase more eBooks or documents, then you will need to do another backup to make sure all the files are on your computer.

Note: *The folder can be saved on your computer's Desktop or inside another folder on your computer. Where you save it depends on how you manage your computer files.*

How to Take Screenshots

Sometimes you see something on your Kindle Paperwhite screen that you just cannot believe, and want to take a screenshot of it in case it disappears later. Likewise, this function can be used for items you would like to share with others, or just for fun. In any event, taking a screenshot with this device is pretty simple especially when compared with other e-Readers on the market.

While you are on the screen you would like to take a screenshot of, place and hold your fingers at the very upper-right hand corner and very lower-left hand corner of your screen at the exact same time. You must be pressing down at the very edge of both corners simultaneously for it to work. Once you are, there will be a quick flash on the screen, as if you have literally taken a picture.

The screenshot will save to your device, and will be available to share when you plug your device into the computer via USB. Open the Kindle device on your computer and you'll see all of your screenshots within the folder.

Note: *You can also use the very upper-left hand corner, and very lower-right hand corner to take a screenshot. The personal preference is yours.*

How to Increase or Decrease Font Size

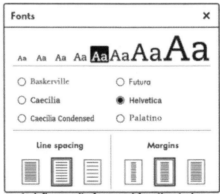

The Kindle Paperwhite has new, hand tuned fonts that account for six styles, and eight adjustable sizes. When you are reading an eBook or document on your device, tap the top of the page/display on your screen. On the far left there will be an "Aa" icon on the toolbar. After you tap this icon, it will allow you to adjust the size and style of font you prefer. You can also adjust line spacing and margins on the document or eBook you are reading. You can change these settings as often as you would like by simply tapping the icon itself. The options will be revealed on your current document as a result.

How to Sync Furthest Page Read Across all Devices

If you have more than one device in which you enjoy books and periodicals, there is an easy way to ensure that no matter which one you are using, you are going to pick up where you left off. All you have to do is ensure that your Whispersync Device Synchronization is turned on. To do so, simply follow these steps.

1. Visit the "Manage Your Kindle" site at Amazon.com.
2. Under Your Account, Click "Manage Your Devices."
3. Locate the "Device Synchronization" and enable the Whispersync setting.

How to Remove an eBook From Your Kindle Paperwhite

Sometimes it just is not necessary to keep everything. When you are ready to remove an eBook from your device, start at the Home page and locate the title you would like to delete. Tap and hold your finger on the title until the menu options are revealed. Tap "Remove from Device" and Voila! The eBook is deleted.

How to Remove Recommended Content

Removing the items that Amazon recommends for you is a simple task.

1. From the Reading toolbar, tap the "Menu" option.
2. Tap "Device Options."
3. Tap the "Personalize Your Kindle" option.
4. Tap "Recommended Content," and change it to its disabled status.

When to Choose Cloud Storage vs. Device Storage

The Kindle Paperwhite only has 2 GB of storage space, and previous Kindle versions have had 4 GB. With a smaller amount of storage space, this device can store roughly 1,100 books. However, Amazon provides Cloud storage, which is free storage space for all your digital purchases. In addition, you can store your own documents on the Cloud.

Basically, if you find that your device has reached its storage capacity, you can delete books from your Kindle Paperwhite, and they will still be stored in your Cloud. Any time you want to read a book you own that is on your Cloud, you simply tap it on your Cloud, and then it will download and open for reading on your Kindle Paperwhite.

Reference books like the Bible, a Dictionary, or other eBooks you often refer to are books you may want to always leave on your device for quick and easy access. However, novels and other books that you are likely to only read once, may be best stored in your Cloud if you are getting close to using your Paperwhite's 2 GB of storage space.

How to Display eBooks as in Cover View or List View

With the Paperwhite, you can view your content in List View, which displays title and author in a list, or Cover View, which displays eBook covers.

To change your view:

1. Tap Menu from the Home screen.
2. Tap List View to view content in list form, or Cover View to see the eBook covers. When you choose Cover View, you will see six eBooks per page.

Note: *Publishers determine cover art. Because of this, some eBooks do not have a cover. Books or documents that do not have a cover will display a book icon.*

Calibre eBook Management

Managing your eBooks is essentially effortless with the Kindle Paperwhite's Collections option. However, when you want to experience more, and receive eBook options that the device does not provide on its own, download the Calibre eBook Management application to enjoy a plethora of device related functionality effortlessly.

First, Calibre allows you to manage your library completely, and allows you to sort and search by title, author, dates (published or added to the library), size, or rating. In addition, it gives you the opportunity to add metadata including tags or comments, to initiate a secondary search level.

Next, it can convert a large number of existing formats into eBooks, so you can enjoy them on your Paperwhite. Gone are the days of your device not supporting a certain file type. Calibre removes the hassle of unsupported formats, including materials from the web, and opens your device up to a new world, and extraordinary amount of material. It then formats the files to read like an eBook, so you get exactly what you expected as a result.

Lastly, Calibre provides users with synching capabilities, as well as a comprehensive eBook viewer options so you can view tables of contents, references, CSS, and customized views.

You can learn more about this helpful web application at the Calibre eBook Management website <http://calibre-ebook.com/>.

Kindle Paperwhite vs. Previous Kindle Versions

The Kindle Paperwhite is the most advanced Kindle Amazon has released to date. The increased battery life, beautiful touch screen, and built in, adjustable light are excellent features. However, if you have owned a previous version of the Kindle e-Reader, you may notice there are some options missing from the Paperwhite that were included on previous versions.

First of all, the Paperwhite only has 2 GB of on board storage space, which holds about 1,100 books. Previous Kindles had 4 GB of space, and they could hold twice as many books. However, Amazon has its Cloud storage service, which stores all your digital content for free.

Another thing that is missing from the Kindle Paperwhite is the audio and Text-to-Speech. The lack of audio has shocked some previous Kindle owners who enjoyed listening to MP3s as background music while they read. The reason Amazon took this feature out is to make the Paperwhite smaller and lighter. If this is something you find you cannot live without, the Kindle Fire and the Kindle Fire HD both include an improved Text-to-Speech function, and they have audio.

All-New Kindle Paperwhite Overview (2013 Version)

Of all the things Amazon does well, with their tablets and Prime service, and their selection of products and electronics, they have once again raised the bar in the e-reader world with the launch of the new, 2013 Kindle Paperwhite. Hitting the shelves -- virtual and otherwise -- the first week of October 2013, the initial response to this exceptional device has been overwhelmingly stellar.

First things first, the new iteration of the Kindle comes in two different version. The standard version is currently priced at $119 USD and includes all of the same features that made the previous versions great including the no-glare screen, even in the sunniest weather, a weight that is 30% lighter than the iPad Mini, and a battery that literally lasts for weeks -- not hours.

So what could Amazon have done to top their already magnificent e-reader? Plenty. Starting with a built-in next generation light that reduces eye strain, which any reader will appreciate. What's more is that the screen's display technology has increased to make whites whiter and blacks blacker, so the contrast is incredibly crisp.

The overall built-in technology has been enhanced as well, allowing for a 19% lighter touch to maneuver through the pages, which can be flipped even quicker for smooth turning and seamless reading potential. Add to the crispness with the ability to read with one hand, thanks to its ideal size, and there is not much you cannot do with this device at the ready.

Of course you can still adjust your text size to fit your reading preference, and carry your entire library with up -- up to 1100 books. There is also an ever-exciting feature called Time to Read, which allows you to assess -- based solely on your personal reading rate -- how long it will take to finish the chapter you are currently on, so there is no more debate as to whether you should put the "book" down, or squeeze the last bit of its intrigue in before moving onto something else. The standard all-new Kindle Paperwhite is listed at 6.7" x 4.6" x 0.36", with a six inch display, and weighs a mere 7.3 ounces. It is completely wireless, and has an internal hard drive of 2GB

Version two of this newly released e-reader is the all-new Kindle Paperwhite 3G! Of course the latter moniker delivers the direct connotation of built-in WIFI, and if you surmised as such you would be correct. Unlike the standard version, where you have to be connected to an external WIFI network in your home, office, coffee shop or random hot spot, the 3G version has WIFI built right in, so there is no need to search the world -- or a every few feet -- to find a hotspot to download books, magazines or newspapers.

The 3G version also incorporates one other change that Amazon touts as being in the works for over two years: a patented front lit design that will allow your eyes to rest effortlessly on the glare-free screen. The size is the same as the standard version, and so are all of the new features that are outlined below. Finally, with its inclusion of WIFI, owners of the 3G version will have access to games and apps, which the standard version does not support. It is completely up to you whether this is a good thing or not. Some people enjoyed the reading concept to be separate from their other devices, allowing a getaway to immerse themselves in a book. Others, well, they like the idea of both. It is your call, buyers. The difference is, of course, the price. The Kindle Paperwhite 3G version goes for $179.

All-New Kindle Paperwhite Features (2013 version)

As with any new technological device, something new is on the horizon for those who want to upgrade to the latest and greatest version. The all-new Kindle Paperwhite provides the same newly adapted features that will have everyone placing this functional and affordable e-reader on their holiday wish lists. To follow is a list of what is new on both devices.

Using Kindle Page Flip

Kindle Page Flip is converting some non-e-readers into possible buyers with this new feature. The complaint has long been that you cannot flip through pages of an eBook with ease -- or precision. The new Page-by-Page feature extinguishes that frustration by placing a slider on the bottom of the "book" that allows the reader to open a new window showing thumbnails of the previous or upcoming pages, without losing the page you are currently on.

Scan by Chapter is another feature that is available in a pop-up window style, so you do not lose your page, and can fast forward or rewind your reading by entire chapters, instead of flipping page after page until you get there. This is a great tool for those who need to reference a certain area of the book without losing their place, or hopelessly scanning the type on each page as they search for what they are looking for.

The pop-up ideology has certainly proven its point of usefulness as far as these new features go, because you never have to leave the page you are on. You can simply scan about the book until you find what you are looking for! The best part, if you ask someone who actually uses them, is when footnotes are involved. You can simply tap on the footnote and it will provide the reference in a pop up, without moving your page or taking you to the end of the book. You only have to journey there if you want to, and you still will not lose your place!

Using Smart Lookup

Smart Lookup has intelligence written all over it, no pun intended. This feature integrates a completely new and enhanced dictionary with X-Ray access and Wikipedia, which is something everyone can use. Here is how they work.

The enhanced dictionary feature is a grown up version, if you will, of the one that was available on the past devices. Although you were always able to tap on a word to get its definition display on the screen, the improved dictionary on the Paperwhite is the complete Oxford English Dictionary. The other difference is, the dictionary segment can work in a tab, with the X-Ray and Wikipedia tabs aligned next to it, for easy toggling on any subject, or it can be used as a standalone book to look up words that you see or hear anywhere. You can also just flip through it, if that is your kind of party. Completely your call.

X-Ray access provides an in depth look at a character, place, historical figure, or topic and how they are listed in the book by showing the passages that included the highlighter word. For example, if you have ever been reading a book, and put it down for a while only to come back and say to yourself, "Who is this Steve character again?" All you have to do is press on the character's name to bring up their bio, and the other areas of the book where he is mentioned, so you can put him back in the proper context. This works, too, for places that may or may not be fictional. When you press on the location, X-Ray will tell you if it really exists and its significance, or if it is fictional and how it fits into the book's make-up. Pretty smart.

Wikipedia access is a blessing with this device, because it keeps you from having to look up an entry for a person, place or thing -- or idea, even -- on your own, through Wikipedia. No one likes to stop reading to look up a name they are certain belongs to someone else they have heard of before, so highlighting their name, and tapping the Wikipedia tab will provide their full information from the actual Wikipedia page. Including whether or not the person you were thinking of is related to the person in question. Problem solved, and you can return to your concentrated reading efforts until the next time.

Using the Vocabulary Builder

This new and exciting feature called Vocabulary Builder could have helped a lot of kids ace their English exams as kids, using the same exact methods parents years ago prescribed: Flash Cards. The only difference is, these flash cards are electronic, and are created for each and every word you look up in the dictionary. After aggregating all of the words in one place, you can flip through the flash cards and quiz yourself on the definitions. Once you have mastered the word, and made it your own, you can mark the flash card as such, and it the Paperwhite internal genius will file it away accordingly. Even if you look up a word that was not in one of your books, using the dictionary's standalone feature, there will be a flash card created for it as well, to help you build your vocabulary into a monstrous wealth of knowledge.

Goodreads Integration (Coming Soon)

Before you can understand what an amazing integration the Goodreads update to the Kindle will be, you first have to understand what Goodreads is. Goodreads is an exceptional offering that provides the social mechanism that has been missing from technology for years. Simply put, it serves as an online book club where individuals can freely search the extensive user populated database of books, reviews and annotations.

Users are able to sign up for free at the Goodreads.com website, and generate a library, catalogs and reading lists, as well as create their own groups -- or online book clubs -- to suggest and discuss certain materials that they have a shared interest in.

Goodreads users can create personal bookshelves, review and rate books, and apply that information to their social media outlets like Facebook. Users can also find out what their friends are reading, and enjoy discussion groups about the same book with people they do not know!

Users can rate books using a five star system, and can even add their very own review to the rating, if they so desire. The site also offers trivia, quizzes and quotations that everyone can enjoy while interacting with the balance of the members.

All of this sounds spectacular to the reader in you, right? Then you will love the fact that Amazon purchased Goodreads and expects to have an update established for this very Kindle by the holiday season. This addition will completely enhance the social experience behind reading great books -- and some not so great -- and sharing your experiences with other. You can also keep a catalog of books you have read, books you want to read, and the ones you are currently reading, so there is never any confusion going forward.

Kindle FreeTime (Coming Soon)

Kindle FreeTime for Paperwhite is the one thing that all parents have been waiting for, as it is no secret that children are enamored with electronic devices. FreeTime allows parents to create profiles on their Paperwhite for their children that are completely personalized. These profiles provide your kids with access to your reading selection as you see fit. So your 14 year old can delve into a mystery novel, while your eight year old can stick with the kids' books for a couple more years, all using the same device.

For encouragement, and just for fun, your young ones will be awarded with achievement badges, allowing the device to keep track of their reading accomplishments. With the device doing all the work, all you have to do is congratulate them on their success, and invite each child to discuss the book with you. This is a fantastic way to interact with kids, and it encourages them to want to read more -- especially if there is an incentive behind the badges.

All you have to do is check the provided progress reports to see the total time they have spent reading, and how many words they have looked up, before assessing the overall number of badges received. This is an exceptional way to understand which words, or types of words, are giving your kids trouble, and to sit down with them and the automatically created flash cards, to help them achieve a broadened vocabulary and comprehension level that will help them in every category of life.

As mentioned briefly earlier the Kindle Paperwhite standard version still provides the dedicated e-reader functionality, so you can get away from the distractions of the world, including the chiming of your other electronic devices, and indulge yourself with a great new read, or an old favorite standby work. This is an awesome side note for parents with kids, as the standard version provides zero opportunity to steel away a few minutes of game time, under the guise of reading.

No matter which device you choose, in this area of electronic majesty, there is no wrong choice. The WIFI will certainly make a difference for someone who does not pass a Starbucks every other block on their way to run errands, or who cannot receive a good signal/service in their home. The entire world has not caught up to the WIFI technology most of the United States enjoys, so it is completely practical to want it within your device. This is a personal decision, and one that does not cost too terribly much more.

With easy access to Amazon's incredible selection, it will take less than sixty seconds to download a book wherever you have WIFI service (with the standard version, or within the 3G version), so you will never be without something to read, which can make all the difference in your sanity on a plane or train. Enjoy the thousands of books stored in the free public domain -- which are just as much yours as they are anyone else's -- or subscribe to magazines, newspapers and periodicals from around the world -- one at a time, or for an entire year. Single issues of just about everything are available through Amazon, including past issues that you may have missed in the mail, before you received your Kindle Paperwhite.

You can also borrow titles for free from Kindle's Lending Library, or access free book samples before buying them if you would like to shop around, and check out genres or writers that you have shied away from in the past. Finally, as Amazon is always famous for, you will be given a list of personalized recommendation reading to choose from, for your convenience. As always, anything you purchase from Amazon will be stored in their Cloud for effortless availability in the future.

This easy to carry, lightweight device can fit almost anywhere, and is optimized for transportability. Just when you thought you would never get to read an entire book again, Amazon comes to your rescue with the all-new Kindle Paperwhite, and Kindle Paperwhite 3G. Your hardest decision now may be deciding which one to get! The seemingly unlimited amount of reading material will be there when you are ready to dive in!

Free eBooks for your Kindle Paperwhite and other Kindle devices

There are plenty of free eBooks to be had for your new Kindle Paperwhite. Below is a list with links provided to different places you can visit online to find free content for your device.

- Amazon's Kindle Store. On the right side of the page, there is a list of the top Paid and Free books for the day. Click on that list, and you will have access to the top free books of the day. http://www.amazon.com/gp/bestsellers/digital-text

- Amazon Kindle Owners Lending Library (for Amazon Prime Subscribers) http://www.amazon.com/gp/feature.html?ie=UTF8& docId=1000739811

- Free Book Feed - http://www.freebookfeed.com

- Many Books - http://manybooks.net/

- Add All eBooks - http://ebooks.addall.com/amazonfree.html

- Bargain eBook Hunter - http://bargainebookhunter.com/category/free/

- Books on the Knob - http://blog.booksontheknob.org/

- Daily Cheap Reads - http://dailycheapreads.com/category/free/

- Daily Free Books - http://www.dailyfreebooks.com/

- e-Reader Café - http://www.thee-Readercafe.com/

- e-Reader Perks - http://www.e-Readerperks.com/

- Free Book Dude - http://www.freebookdude.com/search/label/Kindle?max-results=5

- Pixel Scroll - http://pixelscroll.com/category/ebooks/free-kindle-books/

- Your Daily eBooks - http://www.yourdailyebooks.com/category/free-kindle-books/

Helpful Tip: *You may also want to check with your local library. Many libraries currently offer eBook check out privileges for patrons to borrow various eBooks on Kindle devices.*

Accessories for your Kindle Paperwhite

Although the device operates beautifully on its own, there are a number of functional, fun, and personalization accessories on the market to make your Paperwhite your go-to electronic device. The majority of these helpful Kindle Paperwhite accessories will assist with essentials such as charging the device, or protecting your device and its display screen.

Kindle US Power Adapter

For under $20 you can purchase a power adapter that allows you to attach a USB cord to the Paperwhite, and the opposite end (that usually goes into the computer) into the adapter. The adapter then plugs directly into the wall. No computer necessary. This is perfect for traveling, and even home use, so you can charge your device without turning on your computer.

Kindle Case Cover

It is incredibly important to keep your electronic devices safe from accidental drops, scratches, and spills, which are easily accommodated with the purchase of a Kindle Case Cover. Whether plastic, leather, or synthetic material, designer, trendy or functional, a case will help protect your device when it is not in use. So next time you slide it into your purse or briefcase, the nail file that you forgot about being in that very same bag will not scrape your device.

Kindle Anti-Glare Screen Protector

Although the Kindle Paperwhite is very low on glare as it is, this screen protector provides a bevy of benefits in addition. If you do not have one, you have certainly noticed that your fingerprints are all over the face of your screen – day in and day out. So you clean it, and clean it, and clean it, receiving the same results each time you use it: More fingerprints. The screen protector cuts down on the oil transfer from your hands to the screen, and allows for a cleaner surface and easier to read screen at all times. It is definitely worth the money, as they average around $5 each, and stay in place for quite some time.

Stylus Pen

A stylus pen isn't just for use on tablets like the Kindle Fire HD or Apple iPad. If you want to prevent smudging by way of all the tapping you do with your fingertips, a good stylus pen may be the investment for you to make, in lieu of the screen protector. Stylus pens may make it easier when tap-typing onto your e-Reader display, for when you're using the experimental web browser. The stylus pens can generally be found on Amazon's website for $15 or less.

Amazon Kindle Micro USB Cable

USB cables are a dime a dozen these days, and can be found in just about any drawer in any technologically savvy home. The problem is, you never seem to know when they have gone bad, or stopped working. There is not a light that says so, and you can drive yourself mad trying to figure out why your device will not charge. Do yourself a favor and purchase a brand new one that is made specifically for this device. It is $10, and will provide you with all the confidence in the world in its functionality.

Conclusion

The Kindle Paperwhite is an excellent e-Reader device which can take a bit of getting used to in order to become comfortable with. Due to its lightweight nature and its great features for readability in low or bright light situations, it's perfect to take just about anywhere you want to read. The Paperwhite is sure to provide reading enthusiasts hours of satisfaction in looking at their favorite eBooks, online articles, magazines, or other content.

Refer back to this guide as you continue to learn your way around the device, or find any issues you need to troubleshoot. You can also refer to the Amazon Kindle forum for further help with your device from other Kindle owners.

With the link above you will be able to interact with a community of fellow Kindle owners to get answers to questions, exchange other ideas, and troubleshoot any new issues for the device.

Keep in mind that technology changes fast, but as of right now in early 2013 this guide is something I put extra attention into for the Paperwhite. I hope you have found this guide useful in learning to navigate and use your Paperwhite e-Reader for all its abilities!

More Books by Shelby Johnson

Kindle Fire HD and HDX User's Guide Book: Unleash the Power of Your Tablet!

Facebook for Beginners: Navigating the Social Network

iPad Mini User's Manual: Simple Tips and Tricks to Unleash the Power of Your Tablet!

iPhone 5 (5C & 5S) User's Manual: Tips and Tricks to Unleash the Power of Your Smartphone! (includes iOS 7)

How to Get Rid of Cable TV & Save Money: Watch Digital TV & Live Stream Online Media

Chromecast Dongle User Manual: Guide to Stream to Your TV (w/Extra Tips & Tricks!)

Samsung Galaxy S4 User Manual: Tips & Tricks Guide for Your Phone!

Made in the USA
Lexington, KY
24 November 2014